Moscow & St. Petersburg Travel Guide

Attractions, Eati
Shopping & Pla   *ty*

Nicole Wright

Table of Contents

Moscow

Moscow is the capital of the Russian Federation and its most famous attraction, the Kremlin, is full of historic significance. Architecture from the Russian Empire can still be seen in the city and signs of wealth abound. Moscow was once the capital of the former Soviet Union (USSR) prior to the end of the Cold War.

Stand at the center of Red Square in Moscow and drink in the rich and multilayered life of one of the world's great cities. The colorful onion domes of St. Basil's Cathedral arise to the south in all their vibrant glory.

Turn a quarter-turn to the right, and see Spasskaya Tower, Moscow's version of Big Ben. The tower anchors the southeastern corner of the red stone wall of the Kremlin—center of power for the politicians of modern Russia, as it had been for the commissars of the old Soviet Union and the czars of older Russia.

At the midpoint along the Kremlin wall stands the squat pyramid of Lenin's Tomb—yes, he's still there, even if the Communist empire he created no longer exists. At the north end of the square is the State History Museum.

Rotate a little further right towards the east and there is GUM, at one time the largest department store in the world.

If you had a vantage point on the International Space Station, you could see that Moscow is a city of concentric rings and spokes. The Kremlin and Red Square make up the hub. Through the centuries Muscovites have added walls for protection and roads for mobility as they spread ever outward. Within the vastness of Russia, Moscow is the center of an empire, and the Kremlin is the center of Moscow.

Look at the ordinary people on the streets, on the Metro, at the ballet in this Eurasian metropolis, and you will see stories of survival told on their faces. And you will see pride in who they are. Heroic rootedness in the face of harsh climatic, economic, and political conditions describes the character of Moscow and its people. Everything you see in Moscow tells that story.

Culture

Russians take great pride in their culture and in being cultured. No one would ever want to be considered *nekulturny*—uncultured, uncivilized. In Moscow, you will find many examples of some of the most splendid culture available anywhere.

Not far to the northeast of the Kremlin is Moscow's Theater District. There, on Theater Square, you will find the Bolshoi Theatre and the Maly Theatre. Nearby is Moscow Arts Theater. If you are in Moscow at the right time, check out the Chekhov International Theater Festival.

Do you appreciate the fine arts? Moscow has plenty of museums exhibiting the finest in Russian and international art. The Pushkin Fine Arts Museum is well known for its impressionist and post-impressionist artworks. The Tretyakov Gallery specializes in traditional Russian paintings, and includes a large collection of icons. Be sure to include a visit to the Gorky House Museum—a mansion that was home to the writer Maxim Gorky during the 1930s.

Reminders of the Soviet era appear throughout the city. Buildings constructed during the Stalin regime were known for their blandness: squat, dull, functional, and usually gray. By contrast, many Metro stations provide some of the best examples of Soviet Realism art available in mosaics and statuary. The bitter irony of Soviet Communism may still be seen on Lubyanka Square. On one corner is the infamous former headquarters and dungeon of the Soviet secret police — whether known as the Cheka, the KGB, or an alphabet of initials in between. The dark joke told during the days of the Soviet Union is that the Lubyanka was the tallest building in Moscow — you could see Siberia from its basement. Across the street is "Children's World," Russia's largest toy store.

Location & Orientation

Russia's largest city with a population of over 10.5 million, Moscow sits at the same latitude (55 degrees) as Copenhagen, Denmark, and Edinburgh, Scotland. Moscow is situated on and named for the Moskva River, which flows into the Oka River, which in turn discharges into the Volga River and ultimately into the Caspian Sea. Moscow Standard Time is UTC plus four hours, and observes no daylight savings time changes.

The easiest way to get around Moscow is via its wide-ranging and world class Metro subway system. Look for the large "M" sign. Be sure to obtain city and Metro maps both in English and in Russian. Although finding a Muscovite who speaks English is usually not too difficult, on occasion a non-English speaker might still be able to help you with directions as the two of you work between English and Russian language maps.

Currently, a one-ride Metro ticket will cost you 28 rubles; a thirty-day, unlimited-ride Smart card will cost 1,710 rubles.

Climate & When to Visit

June through July is the main tourist season in Moscow for native Russians. Smart visitors might want to schedule visits in either late spring or early fall when the temperatures are mild. High temperatures in July average around 23 degrees Celsius, while low temperatures in January average around -12 degrees Celsius. Those who don't mind cold weather and snow might well enjoy winter activities in and around Moscow.

Culture addicts will want to visit during June when Moscow hosts the annual International Tchaikovsky Music Competition as well as the annual Moscow International Film Festival.

Sightseeing Highlights

The Kremlin

Near to the Borovitskaya or the Biblioteka imeni Lenina
Metro stations, bordered on the east by Red Square, and
on the south by the Moskva River.
The Kremlin is closed to visitors on Thursdays.
http://www.kreml.ru/en/info/visitors/

The main entrance to the Kremlin is midway along the
wall that faces roughly to the northwest, at the Kutafya
Tower. Ticket offices for the Kremlin, its cathedrals, and
the Armoury are found nearby in the Alexandrovsky
Gardens. Don't try to enter by way of the entrances facing
the Red Square, especially not the one through the famed
Spasskaya Tower: That entrance is for government
officials only.

The Russian word *kremlin* means "fortress," and a series of fortifications have stood on the site of today's Kremlin since possibly as early as the late 11th century. Czars and Soviet leaders have added, altered, and dismantled various palaces, cathedrals, and government buildings over the centuries. Even now in the post-Soviet era, the Kremlin stands as the actual seat as well as the symbolic representation of Russian power and authority. Literally situated at the center of Moscow, truly the Kremlin is the heart of the city and of Russia itself.

A ticket to any of the Kremlin's museum attractions will also permit you to wander much of the grounds. Try at least to see these features within the Kremlin walls:

Cathedral Square

Three cathedrals, a palace, two churches, and a bell tower face Cathedral Square. In the 15th century, all the main streets of Moscow met here. Once used for the coronation of grand dukes, Russian Orthodox patriarchs, and czars, today inaugurations for the President of the Russian Federation are held on the square.

The huge building with the gold cupola to the west of the square is the Grand Kremlin Palace, built in the mid-nineteenth century as the czar's residence. It once served as home of the Supreme Soviet of the USSR.

Moving clockwise, the Palace of Facets and the small Church of Laying Our Lady's Holy Robe give way to the Assumption Cathedral, which is considered the Mother Church of Russia. The present cathedral building was built in the sixteenth century by Grand Duke Ivan III, and is the burial place for most of the Russian Orthodox Metropolitans and Patriarchs. Legend has it that as the German *Wehrmacht* approached Moscow in the winter of 1941, Soviet dictator Joseph Stalin ordered a secret worship service held in the Assumption Cathedral to save the Motherland from the Nazis.

Continuing clockwise and a little behind the Assumption Cathedral is the Patriarch's Palace, with the monstrous, 5.94 meter-long, cast bronze Czar Cannon next to it. Though never used in a war, it may have been fired at least once.

One more turn clockwise brings you to the Ivan the Great Bell Tower, with its Czar Bell, and then to the Archangel's Cathedral. The current Archangel's Cathedral was built in the sixteenth century and served as the burial site for czars and grand princes until Peter the Great.

One last turn to the right takes you to the Cathedral of the Annunciation, which served as the personal chapel of the czars.

Ivan the Great Bell Tower

The Ivan the Great Bell Tower was built in 1508 to serve as the bell tower for the three cathedrals situated on Cathedral Square. Serving also as an observation point, for centuries by imperial decree it was the tallest building in all Moscow. The tower contains twenty-two bells.

Between the Ivan the Great Bell Tower and the Kremlin Wall is the Czar Bell, which is currently the largest bell in the world. Cast from bronze, it was broken during the casting process and has never been rung. It is 6.14 meters high, has a diameter of 6.6 meters, and weighs 201,924 kilograms. The broken piece sitting next to the bell weights 11,500 kilograms.

During the French invasion of 1812, Napoleon Bonaparte wanted to take the Czar Bell back to France as a war trophy, but was unable to do so.

Old Believer Orthodox Christians believe that when Judgment Day arrives, the Czar Bell will be made whole once again and be taken up into heaven, where it will call the faithful to prayer.

Armoury

As its name implies, the Kremlin Armoury began life as the royal arsenal in the early sixteenth century. Over time, master craftsmen were employed at the Armoury to create jewellery, icons, and household items for the royal family. Later, gold and silver treasures of the czars were housed there. In 1806, Czar Alexander I decided to make the Armoury the first public museum in Moscow. In 1960, it was designated as the official museum of the Kremlin.

Unique Russian collection of artistic and historic significance are found today at the Armoury. You may see such items as the Imperial Crown of Russia, the Orloff Diamond, the helmet of Yaroslav II, the ivory throne of Ivan the Terrible, and ten Fabergé eggs.

Red Square

Near to the Okhotny Ryad Metro Station, and outside the northeast wall of the Kremlin

With no vehicular traffic to dodge, you can wander around Red Square as much as you want. Once, a moat had separated the Kremlin from the square, but that was leveled in 1812. Although known as one of the world's great public spaces, Red Square is not among the world's largest squares. At 73,000 square meters, it is not even Moscow's largest square. (Universitetskaya Square in front of Moscow State University has that honor at 130,000 square meters.)

The English name for the square—"Red Square"—arises from a mistranslation of its Russian name, *Krasnaya Ploschad*, which it is said to have gained after the building of St. Basil's Cathedral and the renovation of Spasskaya Tower in the fourteenth and fifteenth centuries. The Russian word *krasnaya* can mean either "red" or "beautiful" in English. Common myths among English-speakers is that Red Square gained its name either because of bloody executions held there, or because of its association with the "Red" Communist government of the USSR, or simply because of the pavement's red color. But none of these is the correct origin of the square's name.

Some truth is contained within these naming myths. Czars—particularly Ivan the Terrible—ordered grisly torture and executions on Red Square. And during the Soviet era, parades of the latest and grandest military hardware in the Red Army arsenal crossed Red Square each May Day and each anniversary of the October Revolution, reminding the world not to mess with the USSR. The Putin government has reinstituted this military spectacle.

Originally red cobblestone, Red Square has been paved with granite since 1930. Come up upon Red Square from the north and pass through the Resurrection Gate. This is a 1990's replica of an arch originally built in the 1530s. Off to the left will be the rebuilt Kazan Cathedral; to your right is the State History Museum.

Walk out onto the square itself. To your left is GUM (pronounced goom)—the State Department Store. To your right is the Kremlin. At the center right side of the square and in front of the Kremlin wall is Lenin's Mausoleum.

Head down to the south end of the square. Just before you reach St. Basil's Cathedral, you'll come upon a 13-meter long stone platform known as the "Place of the Brow" or Place of the Skulls" — or, in Russian, *Lobnoe Mesto*. From this rostrum, Ivan the Terrible is known to have addressed the people of Moscow. Later czars also used it for the issuing of decrees. At times, a temporary altar would be set up on it for use in worship with congregants filling Red Square.

Some will tell you that the platform was used for public executions, but that never happened there. Executions were usually held behind St. Basil's.

Nearby and just to the right of the cathedral is Red Square's only statue. In 1612, Prince Dmitry Pozharsky and a merchant named Kuzma Minin put together a Russian volunteer army that forced out a Polish-Lithuanian army out of Moscow. Their statue once stood at the center of Red Square, but the Communist government moved it in 1936 to make large parades easier.

Look now to the southeast corner of the Kremlin Wall where the Spasskaya Tower stands. Dating from 1491, in the mid-1600s a large Icon of the Savior was mounted on the tower's gate, thus giving it the name, The Savior's Tower, as *spasskaya* is savior in Russian. The gate is now reserved for use by government officials and foreign dignitaries. Throughout Russia, the gate is famous for its clock and chimes. In 1935, the Soviet government replaced the double-headed Russian eagle that had perched upon the tower's pinnacle with a large, lighted red star made of ruby glass. Similar stars were placed on the Troitskaya, Nikolskaya, Borovitskaya, and Vodovzvodnaya towers of the Kremlin wall.

Lenin Mausoleum

On Red Square in front of the east Kremlin wall.

Open every day from 10:00 AM to 1:00 PM, except Mondays, Fridays, and holidays. No admission charge. No cameras or recording devices are permitted. Lockers are provided for checking electronic devices. Expect to be searched before entering. Show respect while in the tomb, and refrain from talking, smoking, placing hands in pockets, or wearing hats. You will be asked to keep moving past Lenin's embalmed body.

See Vladimir Lenin's embalmed body while you can!

When the architect of the 1917 Bolshevik Revolution and founder of the Soviet Union died in 1924, Lenin had left a will mandating that his body should be laid to rest alongside that of his mother in St. Petersburg. The Communist leadership, however, had different ideas. Quickly, they placed his body on display and commissioned an architect to build a suitable structure for public viewing. During the first six weeks after Lenin's death, more than 100,000 people visited his tomb.

Within five years, a method was developed for preserving the body much longer than thought possible. A new and more permanent mausoleum was built, and Lenin's body was placed inside for continued viewing. There Lenin's body has remained except for about four years during World War II, when it removed to Siberia to keep it out of the hands of the Nazis.

Upon his death in 1953, Joseph Stalin became Lenin's tomb-mate, until Nikita Khruschev ordered Stalin removed and buried behind Lenin's Tomb in 1961.

Since the fall of the USSR, Russian politicians and public had debated whether finally to fulfil Lenin's request for his last place of rest. Recent Russian polls show a majority urging removing Lenin from his Red Square mausoleum and burying him in St. Petersburg.

One of the highest honors the Soviet Union could grant its heroes was burial in the ground behind Lenin's Mausoleum or within the Kremlin wall itself. Among the 115 persons entombed in the Kremlin wall are Maxim Gorky, Marshal Georgi Zhukov, cosmonaut Yuri Gagarin, and Alexei Kosygin. Among those buried in individual graves between Lenin's tomb and the Kremlin wall are Felix Dzerzhinsky, Joseph Stalin, Leonid Brezhnev, Yuri Andropov, and Konstantin Chernenko.

St. Basil's Cathedral

Branch of the State Historical Museum
Red Square, Moscow 109012
Tel: +7 (495) 698-33-04
http://www.saintbasil.ru/en/
At the south end of Red Square.

Its real name is the Cathedral of the Protecting Veil of the Mother of God, also known as the Cathedral of St. Vasily the Blessed. Most English-speakers call it St. Basil's Cathedral. It was consecrated in October of 1552, to commemorate the victory of Ivan the Terrible at Kazan. A legend claims that Ivan the Terrible commanded the eyes of its architect be put out so that no edifice so beautiful could ever be built.

After the 1917 Bolshevik Revolution, St. Basil's was seized by the Soviet government, which strongly considered tearing it down to provide a larger southern entrance to Red Square that would be more convenient for large parades. Instead, in 1928, St. Basil's was turned over to the State Historical Museum and was transformed for a time into a museum of atheism. The current Russian Federation continues ownership of St. Basil's as a branch of State Historical Museum and a prime focus of Russian heritage.

No written description can do true justice to the beauty of St. Basil's Cathedral. Nor can a photograph. Only an in-person visit can begin to appreciate it.

Old Arbat Street

Beginning about 800 meters west of the Kremlin walls, and running for about 1.25 kilometers, Arbat Street is one of the oldest and most famous streets in Moscow. Dating from at least the late fifteenth century, it originally stretched through what was then a suburb where trading caravans would congregate. Over time Arbat Street transformed into a preferred haunt of aristocrats and literary figures such as Aleksandr Pushkin and the Tolstoys.

Since the 1980s, Arbat Street has been closed to vehicular traffic. Today, you'll find street performers, restaurants, cafés, souvenir shops, and an assortment of artists.

Some claim that Arbat Street now displays the culture and history of "Moscow in miniature." Others say that Arbat Street is no longer the real Moscow, and doesn't even look Russian anymore.

Novedivichy Convent

1 Novodevichy proyezd
Krasnaya Presnya, Moscow
Tel: 095/246-8526
Get off at the Sportivnaya Metro Station.

The museum is open 10:00 AM to 5:00 PM, Thursdays through Tuesday. The convent is open daily 10:00 AM to 6:00 PM. Closed the last Monday of the month. While the site is officially a museum, it is also an active Russian Orthodox convent.

If you are interested in Russian church architecture, you can find several good examples on the grounds of the Novedivichy Convent. The most notable of its churches is the Cathedral of the Virgin of Smolensk, which was built in the early sixteenth century. The Kremlin's Assumption Cathedral served as its model.

Legend tells that during the French invasion of 1812, Napoleon ordered the Cathedral of the Virgin of Smolensk blown up. However, a nun ran to put out the fuse at the last moment.

During World War II, Red Army observation posts set up on the convent grounds viewed through binoculars the high water mark of the German *Wehrmacht*.

The Novedivichy Cemetery on the convent grounds dates from the late nineteenth century. It gained a new significance in the 1930s when the Soviets demolished a number of Moscow monasteries. This meant that the human remains interred in them had to be transferred to new resting places. The remains of a number of prominent Russian nobles and literary figures were moved to the Novedivichy Cemetery, most notably playwright Anton Chekhov.

Among the 27,000 persons buried there today are Nikolai Gogol, Raisa Gorbachev, Andrei Gromyko, Nikita Khrushchev, Vyacheslav Molotov, Sergei Prokofiev, Dmitri Shostakovich, and Boris Yeltsin.

Today, the Novedivichy Cemetery is almost full and is only used for the most important of burials.

Church of the Ascension & Palace of Czar Alexey Mikhailovich

Kolomenskoye, Permanent expositions are open 11:00 AM to 7:00 PM, except Mondays. The Palace of Czar Alexey Mikhailovich is open 10:00 AM to 7:00 PM on Saturdays and Sundays.
Tel: +7 (495) 232-61-90 or +7 (495) 615-27-68
http://mgomz.com/kolomenskoe

Now within the city limits of Moscow, Kolomenskoye was formerly a country estate of grand dukes and czars, dating back at least to the 1330s.

It was used by imperial families until the Bolshevik Revolution of 1917.

The Church of the Ascension, also known as The White Column, was built in 1532, in honor of the birth of Crown Prince Ivan, later known as "the Terrible." Its form is considered significant as marking the break from Byzantine church architecture to a more native Russian church architecture.

In the seventeenth century, Czar Alexis I built a new wooden palace at Kolomenskoye. This palace had some 250 rooms and was built without using saws, nails, or hooks. Czarina Catherine II ordered it torn down in 1768 to make way for a smaller but more modern palace.

In 2010, the City of Moscow reconstructed Czar Alexis' wooden palace from a surviving scale model.

Thanks to Soviet efforts, Kolomenskoye is home today for many examples of old buildings and items from throughout the former USSR.

Bolshoi Theatre

On Theatre Square, just north of Red Square.
Take the Metro to the Teatralnaya or Okhotnyi Ryad stations.
Telephone for tickets: +7 (495) 455-5555
http://www.bolshoi.ru/en/

The Bolshoi Ballet Company epitomizes the apex of ballet. Ask anyone.

The Bolshoi Theatre is their home, but also hosts operas and concerts. How can anyone visit Moscow without at least once going to the Bolshoi?

The Bolshoi Theatre dates itself to 1776, when Czarina Catherine II granted Prince Pyotr Urusov a ten-year concession for theatre performances and other forms of entertainments common to the time.

The first theatre building under this concession was built in 1780, on Petrovka Street, from which it gained its name, the Petrovsky Theatre. With control of theatre productions moving first to imperial direction and then to the Governor General of Moscow, the decision was made to build a new theatre on what was projected to become Theatre Square. Work began on the building in 1820, with the theatre opening five years later. Its most prominent feature was its portico with eight huge columns, topped by a sculpture of Apollo in a chariot pulled by three horses.

When the new theatre opened in 1825, it became known as the Big Petrovsky Theatre. The word *Big* in Russian is *Bolshoi*. Hence, the *Bolshoi* Theatre. The present building replaced the older one that was destroyed by a fire. Instead of a three-horse drawn chariot, Apollo's chariot boasted four horses, all in bronze. Inside, about 2,300 people could be seated in six tiers. Substantial renovations were undertaken in 2010.

Institute of Russian Realist Art

Take the Metro to the Paveletskaya Station or the Proletarskaya Station, then take Tram No. 35 or 38 to the "Novospassky Most" stop. Enter from Derbenevskaya Street.

Open 11:00 AM to 8:00 PM, Tuesdays through Sunday, except December 31.

Admission for adults is currently 150 rubles.

Novospassky Dvor Business Center, Building 31
7 Derbenevskaya Embankment, Moscow
115114, Russia
Tel. +7 (495) 276-12-12
http://www.rusrealart.ru/en/

The Institute of Russian Realist Art (IRRA) is a private art museum housed in a former cotton-printing factory. Some 500 works of Russian Realist art are displayed over 4,500 square meters on three floors. The exhibits are divided in this way: First floor — art from present-day Russia; Second floor — Soviet art from the second half of the twentieth century; Third floor — Soviet art from the first half of the twentieth century.

The IRRA is one of Moscow's newest museums, having begun in late 2011, around the collection of a Russian businessman, Alexey Ananyev.

Russian Realism as an art school flourished during the second half of the nineteenth century. Artists understood themselves as social critics and sought realistically to depict Russia's social problems, especially the need to abolish serfdom.

Soviet Realism, or Socialist Realism, sought during the twentieth century to promote the ideals of Marxism and Soviet Communism through art. Artists sought to express the spirit of the Russian people, of the proletariat, and of the Communist Party.

Guided tours, a museum shop, and a cafeteria are available.

In the same neighbourhood, you can find the Bakrushin Museum of Theatre, the Esenin Museum, the Visotsky Museum, the State Tretyakov Gallery, and the Moscow International Performing Arts Center. Across the river is the Novospassky Monastery, which dates to the late fifteenth century.

Garden of Fallen Monuments

Take the Metro to the Oktyabrskaya Station or the Park Kultury Station.
Open 9:00 AM to 9:00 PM daily.
Admission is 100 rubles.

Museon Park
Behind the Central House of Artists
10 Krymsky Val, Moscow
+7 (499) 238-5801
www.muzeon.ru (in Russian)

You will find the Garden of Fallen Monuments called a
variety of names: Fallen Monument Park, Sculpture Park
of the Central House of Artists, or Muzeon Park of Arts
(its actual, legal name). As the Soviet Union fell apart in
1991, citizens began tearing down statues of Soviet
leaders, luminaries, and heroes. Many of these statues
were dumped in alleys and other ignoble places
throughout Moscow. For no known reason, some found
their way to Muzeon Park, while others were later hauled
there.

Originally these examples of Soviet Realism statuary were
left in their toppled-over state. Over time, they were
returned to an upright position, and other statues — some
of them of *victims* of the Soviet Communist order — were
installed.

The Garden of Fallen Monuments remains one of the few
places in twenty-first century Moscow where you can
meander through a park and gaze into the stone faces of
the giants of Marxism-Leninism and the Soviet State.

Gorky Park

Close by to the north of the Garden of Fallen Monuments.
Take the Metro to the Park Kultury Station or the
Oktiabrskaya Station.
9 Krymskiy Val, Moscow, 117049, Russia
Open 10:00 AM to 11:00 PM. Most amusement park rides
are closed during the winter.

"Gorky Park" is a lot easier to say than "The Central Park
of Rest and Culture Named After M. Gorky."
Established in 1928, Gorky Park was intended to be a
model park for other Soviet cities to emulate. If you want
to see how some ordinary Muscovites spent their free
time, Gorky Park is the place. While nothing spectacular
by contemporary standards, Gorky Park can be a nice
place to relax, walk, engage in sports, sunbathe, or risk
the amusement park rides. The Green Theater hosts
outdoor concerts and other events during the summer.

Bunker 42

Take the Metro to the Taganskaya Station, then walk
about a block and a half west. Look for a three-story
yellow building that has a green gate with a red star. (The
entrance is camouflaged as part of an old building.)
Open 10:00 AM to 7:00 PM.

Excursions for individuals who are not residents of the Russian Federation can range as high as 13,000 rubles if you are not part of a large group.

11, 5th Kotelnichesky Lane, Moscow
Tel. +7 (495) 500-05-54
http://www.bunker42.com/index.php?lang=en

There is something about Bunker 42 that will likely cause the short hairs on the back of your neck to stand on end. Bunker 42 — formerly known variously as the Tangansky Protected Command Point, as GO-42, as RFQ Tagan, and at least three other designations — was a secret Soviet military complex buried deep below the surface of Moscow.
It was built in 1951, in response to the threat of a nuclear attack from the United States. As many as 3,000 persons could survive there for at least three months if cut off from the outside world. Did you need a reminder of how seriously the Russians feared the possibility of nuclear war?

Bunker 42 is today a combination of Cold War museum and entertainment facility with over 7,000 square meters of floor area located 65 meters underneath Moscow. Excursions, for which the proprietors recommend pre-booking, offer experiences that include films showing how close the world came to World War III, guided tours through the Cold War Museum, photo sessions while you try on uniforms and gas masks, a re-creation of Stalin's bunker and a simulation of a nuclear attack.

Bunker 42 is also available for corporate events, conferences, parties, special programs for children, and weddings. If you prefer, you can sign up for one of the Airsoft games. Airsoft game background stories include: surviving a nuclear attack in the bunker when provisions are available for only half of you to survive; a terrorist-hostage scenario; and zombie-apocalypse.

Recommendations for the Budget Traveler

Places to Stay

Lodging in most of the world's major cities is just plain pricey. Moscow's hotel offerings are no exception. Moreover, keep in mind three other factors as you book your stay in Moscow. First, many of the hotels won't provide room prices on their web pages. They want you to email or fax them with your desired dates and level of room before they let you know how much you can expect to spend. Second, Russia's Communist past means that a large middle-class has not yet had an opportunity to establish itself. You won't find many large chains of hotels and eateries catering to middle-class wallets. The day will come when that will change. Finally, if you are hoping to find lodging close to central Moscow and landmarks like Red Square and the Kremlin, expect to pay a good deal more for anything better than the most basic lodging.

Napoleon Hostel

Maly Zlatoustinsky per. 2, 4th Floor, 101000, Moscow
Tel: +7 (495) 628-6695
http://www.napoleonhostel.com

Take the Metro to the Kitai Gorod Station.

This hostel claims to be just a five-minute walk from Red
Square and the Kremlin.

If you don't mind staying in an 8-bed mixed dorm, the
Napoleon Hostel will only set you back about $22 per
night (plus $30 taxes and fees). Free Wi-Fi is available in
public areas. A multilingual staff will help set you up
with tours and tickets if you wish. Bathrooms are shared.
Free lockers, but bring your own padlock.

Their website claims that Napoleon slept there (at least in
the same building).

Artel Hotel

Teatrainy proezd, 3/3, Moscow, 109012
Tel: (866) 539-0036

This hotel is actually inside of a nightclub, so if you don't
mind loud music after dark, a room at the Artel Hotel
might be for you. Rooms start at about 2,700 rubles. Close
to Red Square and other central Moscow sights, but
expect very small and dark rooms. Free Wi-Fi is available
in public areas.

Complimentary breakfast.

Moscow Day'n'Night Hostel

Luchnikov Lane House 7/4, Building 6, 2nd Floor Apt 50,
Moscow, 101000
Tel: (866) 539-0036

The Moscow Day'n'Night Hostel is about 275 meters from
Lubyanka Square and its Metro Station. Three
guestrooms offer six beds each, with very basic amenities
starting at about 2,400 rubles per night. One restroom and
shower stall for everyone.

Inga Hotels

Tverskaya Street 12, Building 8, 5th Floor, Entrance 17
(Intercom 2b), Moscow, 125009
Tel: (866) 539-0036

Located about 180 meters east of the Pushkinskaya Metro
Station, and about 820 meters northwest of Red Square.

At the Inga Hotels, an economy twin room with shared
bedroom can be stayed in for starting around 2,610 rubles.
Free Wi-Fi is available in public areas. Flatscreen TV with
cable channels and DVD players are in guestrooms. All
units have basic kitchens.

A la Russ Hotel-Hostel

5 Voznesenskiy St, Moscow
Tel: (866) 539-0036

Another hostel within range of Red Square and the
Kremlin, A la Russ Hotel-Hostel is about 550 meters to
the north of the Arbatskaya Metro Station and about 730
meters northwest of Red Square.

Completely renovated in July 2011, A la Russ Hotel-
Hostel features guestrooms starting at about 2,700 rubles.
Each of the thirty-five guestroom feature televisions with
DVD players, desks, phones, and have basic kitchens.
Free Wi-Fi is available in public areas.

iVan Hostel

Petrovskiy Pereulok 1/30 App 23, Moscow 107031
Tel: (866) 539-0036

The iVan Hostel is within about 180 meters of either the
Pushkinskaya or the Chekhovskaya Metro Station.
Accommodations begin at around 3,015 rubles. Shared
bathrooms and kitchens are the norm. Rooms have LCD
televisions with premium cable channels, free movies,
and DVD players, in case you are too worn out to sightsee
anymore.

The iVan Hostel was completely renovated in 2010.

Places to Eat

Elki Palki

ul. Neglinaya 8/10, Moscow
Tel: (495) 628-5525
www.elki-palki-ru

Take the Metro to the Kuznetsky Most Station.

At this chain restaurant featuring Russian food, you can ask for an English language menu. A meal and drink will set you back about 300 rubles. If you don't know what else to order, you can always try the borscht.

Every Elki Palki restaurant is designed to look like a traditional Russian village hut.

Grabli

Pyatnitskaya ul., 27, Moscow
Tel: (495) 545-0830
www.grably.ru

Grabli is another nice but affordable restaurant, where a good meal for their buffet line will cost you about 300 rubles. For this location of Grabli, take the Metro to either the Tretyakovskaya or the Novokuznetskaya Station.

Noah's Ark

9 Maly Ivanovsky Lane
Tel: (495) 917-0717

Take the Metro to the Kitay-Gorod Station.

Noah's Ark features Armenian cusine. Grilled veal sirloin, marinated in honey, black pepper, and olive oil, then wrapped in grape leaves costs 580 rubles. A traditional style beef kebab costs 680 rubles. Or you might prefer one of the soups, like their forest mushroom soup, or fish solyanka featuring sturgeon and salmon, or the tsar fish soup, seasoned with vodka.

Stolovaya No. 57

Inside the GUM State Department Store on Red Square, 3rd line, 3rd floor.
Tel: (495) 620-3129
Open from 10:00 AM to 10:00 PM
http://www.gum.ru/en/projects/s57/

Stolovaya No. 57 is where Muscovites go to eat when they become nostalgic for the old days of the Soviet Union. *Stolovaya* is Russian for "workers' cafeteria." Good, basic Soviet cuisine is prepared according to the recipes of *The Book of Healthy and Tasty Food.* You can find pickled herring, stroganoff, and more exotic fare such as "herring under a fur coat," which is actually a layered salad of fish, shredded beets, and carrots. Prices are a bargain, as you might expect at a workers' paradise.

Places to Shop

GUM State Department Store

On the east side of Red Square, facing the Kremlin.
Open 10:00 AM to 10:00 PM.
Tel: (495) 788-4343
http://www.gum.ru/en/

From its origins in the trading stalls on Red Square, through the grand commercial building of the nineteenth century, through the Soviet years when plans were made many times to demolish it, through its rebirth as a state-owned, state-run department store in 1953, to its current state of the art complex, GUM has been the first place to shop when in Moscow.

The Soviet days have been left behind, as you will now find shops on the three levels inside of GUM bearing names such as Dior, Armani, Louis Vuitton, Mont Blanc, and Calvin Klein. Yet reminders of those same Soviet days remain in other shops, such as Gastronome No. 1 (Grocery Store), and the Stolovaya No. 57 and Café Festivalnoe restaurants.

Izmailovsky Market

73 Izmailovskoye Highway
Tel: (499) 166-5031
On Saturdays and Sundays, the Vernisage—a large,
outdoor flea market is open for business.

Travel east on the Metro from Moscow's city center and
exit at the Partizanskaya Station.

Because the Izmailovsky Market is some distance away
from the center of things in Moscow, bargains are more
likely to be found. Because of its flea market nature, you
might also find unusual souvenirs to take back home.
Handcrafted matryoshka dolls, black lacquered wooden
boxes, and Soviet era memorabilia are just some of the
items you might find at fair prices with a little bit of
haggling.

St. Petersburg

Located on the Gulf of Finland and the Baltic Sea, the Russian city of St Petersburg is one of the most attractive cities in Russia and is a UNESCO World Heritage Site. Founded in 1703 by Tsar Peter the Great, St Petersburg is the second largest city in Russia and has stunning architecture and rich historical significance.

The city is dotted with numerous palaces, cathedrals, museums, bridges, theaters, parks, and monuments, each an attraction in itself. St Petersburg is a picture postcard city that is loved by visitors of all ages and interests.

The city, on the banks of the River Neva, was originally named St Petersburg to honor the founder. The name was changed to Petrograd in 1914 during World War I. 10 years later on Jan 26, 1924, the city was renamed Leningrad, 5 days after the passing away of its most famous son – Vladimir Lenin. After the disintegration of the USSR, an official referendum was passed to rename the city with its original moniker – St Petersburg.

The city has earned a number of nicknames over the years. It is known as the Venice of the North for its innumerable canals and bridges. The nickname Northern Capital of Russia comes from the age old rivalry with the city of Moscow. It is also known as the City of White Nights for the natural phenomenon of having daylight during the night hours in the summer months. St Petersburg is located on a number of islands on the Neva delta making it also the "City on 101 Islands".

The history of the city is as colorful as its present. The original inhabitants of the region were the Swedes who built a fort to strengthen their presence. Tsar Peter the Great, looking for a seaport to improve his maritime relations, captured the Swedish fort in 1703 and founded the present city. He also constructed the Peter and Paul Fortress, the city's first stone and brick building. In less than a decade he moved the capital from Moscow to St Petersburg.

After a devastating fire in the mid 18th century, restoration and rebuilding started which saw many stunning Baroque architecture being built across the city – many of which are still preserved and open to the public. The 19th and 20th centuries saw a growth of the poor peasant and labor population in the city, triggering the globally historic October Revolution when Lenin stormed the Winter Palace. The seat of the government was moved to Moscow during the World War I (in 1917) when St Petersburg was threatened with German bombing. The city did come under German siege in World War II from September 1941 to January 1944, making it the longest wartime siege of a major cosmopolitan city. It took many years for the city to rebuild itself from the ravages of the World War II which not only depopulated the city but also killed over a million civilians.

Modern day St Petersburg has risen from the turmoil of the numerous revolutions and wars. The sprawling city today showcases its history through its stunning architecture and over 200 museums in and around the city. Skyscrapers and modern day architecture herald the commercial and financial growth of St Petersburg. Art, music, and theater that have been nurtured for hundreds of years still draw the purists to this city. The cityscape is one of the most beautiful in the world. In fact, St Petersburg is also stunning underground, with opulently ornate subway stations decorated with marble and bronze. With so much to see and so much to do, there is never a dull moment in St Petersburg.

Culture

Music and the arts are intrinsically intertwined with the history and culture of St Petersburg. The city has a number of theaters and galleries, some dating back to the 19th century. The Mariinsky Theater - http://www.mariinsky.ru, built in 1860, is an institution in itself. This opera house, also known as the Kirov Ballet, has hosted some of the greatest ballet dancers like Anna Pavlova. Built at the site of the Circus Theater which was destroyed in a fire in 1859, the Mariinsky, named after the wife of Tsar Alexander II, soon rose into prominence not only for the fine performances it hosted, but also for the grandeur of the building. Other theaters in the city include the 19th century Mikhailovsky Theater - http://www.mikhailovsky.ru; and the stunningly beautiful St Petersburg Opera Company - http://www.stpeteopera.org.

Lovers of classical music can head to the internationally popular St Petersburg Philharmonic Grand Hall or the Jazz Philharmonic Hall. The city also hosts a number of pop and rock concerts across a number of venues, the most popular being the Oktyabrskiy Concert Hall and the Ice Palace.

The city has featured time and again in many novels, poems, and movies over the centuries – sometimes reflecting the hardships and inhuman mechanism that grasped the city in its growing years. Most prominent of the authors include Dostoyevsky, Gogol, and Pushkin. It has featured in major films like the Goldeneye (1995), Midnight in St Petersburg (1996) and Anna Karenina (1997).

Location & Orientation

St Petersburg, being a major port city, is well connected by different modes of transport. It is located about 300 km from 2 capital cities – Helsinki (Finland) and Tallinn (Estonia), but is at a distance of over 700 km from the Russian capital Moscow.

The city is served by the Pulkova Airport (IATA: LED) - http://www.pulkovoairport.ru. However, it is to be noted that there is Pulkova 1 Airport (about 17 km from the city) for domestic flights and Pulkova 2 Airport (5 km from Pulkova 1) for the International flights. The Pulkova 2 has many direct connections with a host of cities across the globe. From the airport one can enter the city either by the public bus or taxi. The bus leaves every 8 minutes for the 30 minute journey to the Moskovskaya metro station, from where a train ride to the city center takes about 15 minutes. One can also get down at the Aeroport Railway Terminal to take a commuter train to the city center (18 min) although the frequency of the train is lower (hourly) than the bus. Taxis are available near the arrival terminal and have a fixed rate chart to different parts of the city. It takes about 30 min to an hour by taxi to the city center, depending on traffic.

For those looking for low cost carrier options can choose the Lappeenranta Airport (IATA: LPP) - http://www.finavia.fi/en/lappeenranta/, in Finland. It is located close to the international border, and is about a 6 hr drive from St Petersburg. This small airport has bus (6 hrs) and rail (2 hrs) connections to St Petersburg.

Being a major railway hub, St Petersburg is well connected by train services with a number of Baltic and central European cities. One has to choose from 5 stations in the city – Moskovskii (for Moscow, Ukraine, etc); Vitebskii (for central and east European cities); Baltiskii (for airport bus and rail transfers); Ladozhskii (for Kazakhstan, Helsinki, etc); and Finliandskii (for high speed connection to Helsinki). All these stations have a metro line.

Bus is a cheap option to get to St Petersburg with many major carriers operating frequent connections. Eurolines - http://www.eurolines-travel.com/; Lux Express - http://www.luxexpress.eu/; and Ecolines - http://ecolines.net/en/ - are popular European carriers with multiple connections with St Petersburg. The St Petersburg Central Bus Station is located near the Obvodny Kanal Metro Station, just 2 stops away from the city center.

Being a port city, St Petersburg can also be reached by ferry. Ferry services are offered by a number of companies in Russia, Estonia, and Finland including Finnlines - http://www.finnlines.com and St Peter Line - http://www.stpeterline.com/en/OnBoard/News.aspx. It is also a favorite stop for all major cruise lines with a Scandinavian package. It is interesting to note that one does not need a Russian visa to enter St Petersburg if travelling with a cruise tour.

Once in the city, there are many modes of transport to choose from. There is a good and cheap 5-line metro network; it costs 28 rubles irrespective of the distance, but an extra ticket is needed for a large baggage. One should take at least one trip in the metro to experience the grandeur of the stations. Surface public transport includes the bus, tram, trolleybus, and the marshrutka – minibus plying on a fixed route. Marshrutka vans are identifiable by the letter 'K' and are white or yellow in color. When using the public transport, it is best to have a clear idea of the destination as the conductor often may not speak English. Carrying change is recommended – about 25 rubles per trip per person within the city limits.

Taxis are available all over the city but it is recommended to have an idea of the fare from the hotel or from a local as many taxis run a tampered meter – especially the ones near the Hermitage. It is best to negotiate a flat fare before taking a taxi. One can also use the Call Cab service; a list of call taxis can be found at - http://www.saint-petersburg.com/transport/taxi/taxi-companies/.

An interesting mode of transport and a great way to enjoy the city skyline is to take the aquabus or water taxi. Operating from June to October, there are 3 lines with a fixed timetable. Tourists are often seen taking the aquabus from one end of the line to the other using a mode of transport that was a favorite to the founding father of the city – Tsar Peter the Great.

Climate & When to Visit

St Petersburg has a humid continental climate with warm short summers and long wet winters. April and May sees warm temperatures but snow is not uncommon. June to September sees good weather with occasional rain and low humidity. This is also the peak tourist season. Daytime temperature reaches a high of around 22 degrees Celsius and it falls to the low teens in the night. Winter settles between November and March when daytime temperatures reach a high of 2 degrees Celsius and nighttime sees a fall to 9 degrees below freezing.

Sightseeing Highlights

Hermitage Museum & Winter Palace

34, Dvortsovaya Naberezhnaya / 2
Dvortsovaya Ploschad (Palace Square)
St Petersburg
Tel: +7 812 571 3420
http://www.hermitagemuseum.org

The Hermitage, with over 3 million exhibits from across
the globe, is regarded as one of the leading museums in
the world.

The architectural ensemble that houses this renowned museum consists of the stunning Winter Palace, The Small, Old and New Hermitage, the Hermitage Theater, the Menshikov Palace, and the Museum of the Imperial Porcelain Factory. Founded in 1764 by Catherine II the Great with her private collections, it is one of the oldest museums in the world. By the end of the 19th century, the museum made enough acquisitions to make it one of the largest in the world. Presently, the Hermitage is credited with the largest collection of paintings in the world. The 350-room museum, with nearly 3 million visitors annually, is one of the most visited museums across the globe.

The museum has a wide collection of antiques and artworks, some created by the most notable artists of the period. Only a small portion of the collection is put on permanent display; many are exhibited through various special exhibits throughout the year.

Amongst the different categories of collections, one of the oldest is the Egyptian antiques section. Mesopotamian antiques from ancient Babylon are the highlight of this section. The Classical Antiquities on the ground floor of the New and Old Hermitage buildings have Greek artifacts from 5BC to 3BC that includes pottery, jewelry, sculptures, and monuments.

The Museum has a vast collection of artwork – Prehistoric Art in the Winter Palace has collections from the Paleolithic Age to the Iron Age. The Italian Renaissance and Spanish Art sections in the Old and New Hermitage Buildings have works of some of the greatest masters including Leonardo da Vinci, Raphael, Michelangelo, Goya, Veronese, and Titian. The skylight room with decorated ceilings and red walls add to the beauty of the artworks. Dutch, Flemish, British, French, German, and Russian paintings are also exhibited – many of those created between the 15th and 18th centuries.

The Numismatics and Arsenal Section can be seen in the Knights Hall in the New Hermitage. The 1st floor of the Winter Palace is dedicated to Russian Art. The only portion of the 2nd floor of the Winter Palace that is open to the public exhibits Neoclassical Art of masters including Renoir, Van Gogh, Monet, and Gauguin.

The Museum is housed in many separate buildings, the most striking of which is undoubtedly the Winter Palace. The present building, completed in the 2nd half of the 18th century, can be called as the 4th version of the Winter Palace. The first was a 1708 wood building for Peter the Great. The 2nd was a 1711 stone building that was replaced by the Hermitage Theater (part of the palace was restored and is open to the public). The 3rd, completed in 1735 served as the royal residence for only 17 years before the building of the present Palace was commissioned.

Planning and execution was done to reflect the might of the Russian Empire. At 22 m, it has remained the tallest building in the historic center of St Petersburg. The richly ornate façade that is seen today is almost unchanged although the interiors have gone through many restorations and renovations. The Palace became a part of the Hermitage from 1917 enabling visitors from across the globe to witness the opulence and might of the Russian monarchy during the 18th and 19th centuries.

The dominating neoclassical crescent shaped General Staff Building became a part of the Hermitage in 1993. Built in 1827, the building was originally the office of the Foreign Ministry and the Finance Ministry of the Tsar. It has an interesting collection of wartime uniform and regalia. The Menshikov Palace (RUB 60 and free admission on first Friday of each month) near the Vasileostrovskaya Metro station is also a part of the Hermitage. Built in the early 18th century as the residence of Prince Menshikov, it is the only surviving private residence from that period. The palace is not wheelchair accessible.

Such is the elegance of the palace that it was the center of cultural and social life in the 1st quarter of the 18th century and hosted many royal balls and events. Today, it is completely restored and houses many exhibits including the private collections of the Menshikov family. The Hermitage Storage Facility (Staraya Derevnya Metro) covers 35000 sq m and presently covers a km of displays!

Only guided tours are allowed – 11am, 1pm, 1:30pm and 3:30pm from Wednesday to Saturday. It is closed on Mondays and Tuesdays. The Museum of Porcelain (RUB 60) near the Lomonosovskaya Metro is part of the Hermitage since 2001 and linked with the famous International Porcelain Factory. Established in 1844 its collections grew with a decree that all royal porcelain items must create a replica for the museum. Visitors can head to the Konstantinovsky Palace (RUB 270) - http://www.konstantinpalace.ru/ for the permanent exhibitions. This richly decorated palace has exhibits from Russian history. The Hermitage Theatre, once the private theater of Catherine the Great is a must visit for theater lovers, especially in the summer months when the Mariinsky is closed. The fine performances and the richly decorated interior compete with each other for attention.

The main building of the Hermitage – the Winter Palace – is open Tues to Sun from 10:30 am to 5:30 pm (closes 9:00 pm on Wednesdays). The Palace is near the Admiralteyskaya Metro.

There is an entry fee of RUB 400.

Vasilievsky Island

Located across the River Neva from the Winter Palace, the Vasilievsky Island is the largest island of St Petersburg and easily reachable by foot across the Dvortsovy Bridge. The island has a number of attractions and one can easily spend the better part of the day even with a casual stroll. The Vasileostrovskaya and Primorskaya Metro stations serve the island; one can also choose the bus or tram service.

Naval Museum & Old Stock Exchange

One of the most dominating buildings on the Spit (Strelka) - the easternmost tip of the island - is the former St Petersburg Stock Exchange with its rostral columns. Built in 1810 resembling the Greek Temple of Hera the building is an example of Greek Revival architecture. The rostral columns were added a year later in 1811. The building presently houses the Naval Museum – one of the largest naval museums in the world. The Museum has a large collection of items from the Russian navy especially from World War II. There is an entry fee of RUB 320 for foreigners.

Andreyevsky Cathedral

http://andrew-sobor.ru/

Built in 1720, the Andreyevsky Cathedral is regarded by many as most beautiful church on the island. The present pink and white Baroque styled church replaced the original wooden church that was commissioned by Peter the Great. 2 cathedrals were added to the Church in the 19th century. The Church was severely damaged in bombing and shelling during the Siege of Leningrad but has since been restored to its original glory. The Cathedral is close to the Menshikov Palace and is open from 9:00 am to 7:00 pm.

The Twelve Colleges at St Petersburg State University

Built in 1742 by renowned architect Domeniko Trezini, the Twelve Colleges is a set of 12 identical 3-storey buildings in a neoclassical style of architecture. Originally constructed as 12 separate buildings, it is today one long connected complex stretching 400m in length. The building stood out during its construction as it had a facade that was not river-facing like the other buildings.

The buildings were originally used as trading premises and government offices and were made a part of the Pedagogical Institute (precursor to the University) in 1804. Today, the Twelve Colleges house the Admissions Office and the Faculties of the Earth Sciences and Geological Departments of the University that has, amongst its alumni, 8 Nobel Prize Winners and the Russian President – Vladimir Putin. Visitors have access to some of the Halls of the Twelve Colleges which are, at times, used as venues for classical music concerts. It is closed on Sundays.

Erata

The Erata Museum and Galleries of Contemporary Art - http://www.erarta.com - is the largest private museum of contemporary art in the country. The name Erata is a combination of 2 words – era and arta, which in Russian means the Era of Art. The aim of this institute is to popularize, promote, and encourage contemporary art and artists across the country. Presently, it has about 2300 artworks by 170 artists from all corners of Russia. The span of the project is not limited to Russia and one can find Erata galleries in New York, Zurich, London, and Hong Kong. One can also order artwork online at http://www.erartagalleries.com/.

Different art forms are represented in the collection that includes paintings, sculptures, installation, science art, and video art. The Erata complex also includes 2 cinema halls (for project screenings), a workshop, an art shop, a gift store, a restaurant, and a café. Entry ticket for an adult costs RUB 300 – discounted tickets are available. The Erata is open from 10:00 am to 10:00 pm.

Kunstkamera

The majestic Petrine Baroque building with a turret on the bank of the Neva is the Kunstkamera - http://www.kunstkamera.ru - the first museum in Russia. Established in 1727 with the patronage of Tsar Peter the Great, the building today houses the Peter the Great Museum of Anthropology and Ethnography with a collection of over 2 million objects. The Museum, according to the directions of Peter is dedicated at preserving the curiosities and rarities of the human and natural world. This was done to encourage the research on deformities and to debunk superstitions and myths.

In 1878, the Museum was merged with the Museum of Ethnography and the first exhibition of the unified museum was opened in 1889.

The Museum has 5 levels. The first 3 levels have exhibits from different regions of the world; the top 2 levels have the astronomical displays and the Great Gottorp Globe – a 17th century planetarium. The Museum also has a number of temporary exhibitions throughout the year.

The Kunstkamera is open from 11:00 am to 6:00 pm with an extended hour in the summer months. It is closed on Mondays. The entry fee for a foreigner adult is RUB 250; there are discounts for children, students, and pensioners.

Ancient Theban Sphinxes

One of the most notable sights is 2 sphinxes located across the Academy of Arts building along the quay. These are original granite sphinxes that are over 3500 years old that were excavated in 1820 in a temple site near Thebes. Tsar Peter the Great purchased the sphinxes and had those installed and displayed from 1834. Such is the popularity of these statues that there are six more identical sphinxes sculpted by Russian artists that can be found in the city.

Walking on the streets of Vasilievsky Island, one will find many more interesting sights and attractions. The Zoology Museum - http://www.zin.ru/museum/ - has over 17 million objects; of the half a million that are put on display, one can see the world's only stuffed mammoth and a fully preserved skeleton of a blue whale – the largest mammal in the world. The Mining Institute Museum is one of the largest and oldest of its kind and is housed in an impressive 19th century façade. There are 2 museum ships Krassin - http://www.krassin.ru/en/ and Narodovolets Submarine D-2. The island is also dotted with a number of impressive churches including the Gothic styled St Michael's and the multi-domed Church of Our Lady the Merciful. A stroll to the inner streets can take one to a number of orthodox and Lutheran churches.

The island may not be the best for shopping but there are a number of authentic souvenir shops in the Naval Museum and at the Academy of Arts. There is also a duty free store at the harbor terminal.

Peter & Paul Fortress

The original citadel of St Petersburg, the Peter and Paul Fortress was founded in 1703 by Tsar Peter the Great. It is today an important and integral part of the State Museum of St Petersburg. Originally built with earth and timber during the Northern War, it was soon replaced by a stronger stone building – making it the first completed structure in the city.

The Fortress not only fulfilled many martial purposes, it also served as a prison for prominent political prisoners earning it the nickname – Russian Bastille. Famous personalities who have been incarcerated in its cells include Fyodor Dostoevsky, Leon Trotsky, and Josip Broz Tito.

The most dominating building in the fort compound is undoubtedly the Peter and Paul Cathedral; an orthodox church built in 1733 and dedicated to Peter and Paul, the patron saints of the city and the fortress. The church has a 404ft high golden spire making it the tallest Orthodox Church in the world. On the top of the spire is an angel holding a cross – one of the most important symbols of St Petersburg. The Cathedral is also the burial ground to the Imperial family of Russia including that of Peter the Great, Nicholas II, and Catherine the Great. While the exterior of the Cathedral is dominated by the iconic bell tower with a French carillon, the interior is richly decorated with a mosaic ceiling, painted walls, exquisitely ornate doors, and stained-glass windows.

The fortress compound (6:00 am to 10:00 pm) and all exhibitions (10:00 am to 6:00 pm) are open Thursday to Tuesday. There is a combined ticket for all attractions for RUB 370.

Church of the Savior on Blood

The Russian Orthodox Church of the Savior on Spilled Blood, or, officially the Cathedral of the Resurrection of Christ, was completed in 1907 and is today one of the most visited attractions in St Petersburg. Funded primarily by the Imperial Family, the Church is built at the site where Emperor Alexander II was mortally wounded in a bomb attack. The Church, which was reopened in 1997, after nearly 3 decades of restoration has incredibly detailed artwork that would mesmerize any visitor. It has 7000 sq m of decorated mosaic, claimed to be the most inside any church in the world.

The Church stands out with its romantic nationalism style of architecture. The golden and turquoise onion domes and a richly decorated façade add to the beauty and uniqueness to its looks. The Church is embellished with semi-precious stones like topaz and lazurite. As it was not consecrated after its reopening, the Church is not a recognized place of worship; it is more popular as a mosaic museum.

There is an entry fee of RUB 250 which also allows photography without a tripod.

St. Alexander Nevsky Monastery

Founded in 1710 by Peter I, the St Alexander Nevsky Monastery is the site of some of the oldest buildings in St Petersburg; it is also the burial site of some of the most prominent personalities of Russian culture.

The monastery was built to commemorate the victory of Prince Alexander Nevsky in the Battle of Neva in 1240; it was also built to house the relics of St Alexander Nevsky, the patron saint of the new Russian capital. In the late 18th century it was raised to the rank of a lavra – a compound with a church and cells for the hermits – putting it at par with only two other lavras under the Russian Church – the Trinity Monastery of St Sergius and the Kiev Monastery of the Caves. The Nevsky Monastery had 16 churches in its complex by the beginning of the 20th century, out of which only 5 survive today.

The Monastery burial grounds – the Tikhvin and Lazarus Cemeteries - have the graves of some of the most famous names in Russian art and culture including Tchaikovsky, Dostoevsky, Mikhail Glinka, Anton Rubinstein, and Leonhard Euler.

Bridges on the River Neva

The Venice of the North – St Petersburg – is known for its innumerable bridges and canals. There are 342 bridges across the river and canals within the city limits, not counting the many smaller ones that one may see across the ponds and lakes!

Names of the bridges is as interesting as their count, some are named after the country from which the style of architecture has been taken (French, Italian, etc), some are named after famous personalities (Peter, Nevsky, etc), some others are named after the nearest landmarks (church, bank, etc), while some bridges are just referred to by their color! If lined one after the other, these city bridges will stretch for nearly 16 km.

Some of the most famous bridges include the Bolshoi Obukhovsky Bridge – built in 2004, it is the newest in the list and the only one that is not a drawbridge. With a length of 2824m, it is the longest on the Neva. The widest is the early 19th century Blue Bridge across the Moika. With a width of 97.3m, it is claimed to be widest in the world by some sources. The early 20th century Trinity Bridge is an artwork in granite and iron built in the art nouveau style. The 1916 Palace Bridge near the Winter Palace is most frequented by tourists and is one of the most photographed in the city, especially when it is drawn in the night.

Many of the bridges are lighted up after sundown. A casual stroll in the city streets will take one across many of the bridges, some decorated with statues (Anichkov Bridge), while others merely serving the purpose, but each one contributing to the magical beauty of St Petersburg.

Artillery Museum

http://www.artillery-museum.ru/en

The Military Historical Museum of Artillery, Engineers and Signal Corps or the Artillery Museum, is a state owned museum exhibiting items of the Russian military and those related to the Defense Ministry. Founded in 1703 by Peter the Great, the Museum today not only displays items belonging to the Russian military from over the years, but also arms and weapons captured in various battles and wars.

Collections of the Museum include a copy of the chronicle of the Russian Emperor's Army; cannons used by the army of Tsar Peter the Great, rocket launcher from World War I, a number of the famous Russian export Kalashnikov rifles, and numerous armored vehicles, tanks, missiles, and artillery pieces. It also includes gifts, medals, and honors received by the Russian military. There are a number of guided general and special tours, details of which can be found in the website.

The Museum is open Wednesday to Sunday from 11:00 am to 6:00 pm. It is closed on Monday, Tuesday, and the last Thursday of every month. There is an entry fee of RUB 300; discounted tickets are available for children and groups.

Palace Square

The city of St Petersburg has many squares but the most grandiose of those is certainly the mid 18th century Palace Square at the historic center. Built according to the wish of Empress Elizabeth to showcase the power and authority of the Russian monarchy, the square is not only known for its flamboyance but also for being witness to many historic events including the October Revolution and Bloody Sunday.

The most celebrated building of the Palace Square is the Winter Palace that served as a residence to the Russian monarchy. It was a built in a Russian baroque style, different from the rest of the square which is built in a neoclassical style. The other end of the square has the crescent shaped General Staff Building that was constructed in the early 19th century.

In the middle of the square is a 47.5m high Alexander Column – a single-piece red granite column with a bronze statue - the tallest column of its type in the world. The Palace Square is a popular venue for many music concerts and has featured artists like Madonna, Rolling Stones, Paul McCartney, and Shakira.

St Isaac's Cathedral & Museum

Built in 1858 after a 40 year construction, the Russian Orthodox St Isaac's Cathedral is one of the most visited tourist attractions in the city of St Petersburg.
It is dedicated to the patron saint to Tsar Peter the Great. When completed, it was the main church of the city and the largest in Russia. The gilded dome remains one of the most impressive landmarks of the city.

The Church, with its massive red granite columns, detailed mosaic icons, and stunningly ornate interior could accommodate 14000 worshippers. However, the Church was turned into a museum in 1930 – Museum of the History of Religion and Atheism. The Church remains a Museum as of date but attracts millions of tourists for its sheer beauty, intricate artwork, and elegance.

It is open from 10:00 am to 7:00 pm every day except Wednesday with extended hours (10:00pm) in summer months. There is an entry fee of RUB 250.

Kazan Cathedral

http://kazansky-spb.ru/

Located close to the Nevsky Prospect, the historic avenue of St Petersburg, the Kazan Cathedral is an early 19th century dominating crescent shaped building. Inspired by the Basilica in Rome, the Orthodox Kazan Cathedral became a symbol of victory as the Russian army defeated Napoleon within a year of its construction. The impressive and huge stone colonnade is dedicated to the Our Lady of Kazan who was regarded as a miracle-making icon.

However, like many other religious monuments, the cathedral was closed for service and transformed into a museum in the 1930s. It housed the Museum of the History of Religion and Atheism. Recently, religious services have resumed alongside the existence of the museum although the word 'Atheist' has been dropped from its name. A visit to the Cathedral is a must as for its beauty in its enormity. A lighted Kazan Cathedral in the nighttime is especially beautiful.

Recommendations for the Budget Traveller

Places to Stay

Alexander House Hotel

27 Kryukov Canal Embankment
St Petersburg
Tel: +7 812 334 3540
http://a-house.ru/en/

Located close to the Mariinsky Theater near the Sennaya Ploshad Metro, this family run guesthouse is housed in an 1826 restored building with 20 guestrooms. It is within walking distance to most of the attractions of the city centre. All the 20 rooms have been restored with a different look and the hotel promises an old world charm with modern facilities. The rooms are equipped with cable TV, high speed Internet and telephone. There is a multi-lingual staff.

The Deluxe rooms come with a kitchenette. Room rates start from RUB1800 per night and are free for children under 7 years. There is buffet breakfast in the Hotel's restaurant.

Comfort 10 Hotel

25 Bolshaya Morskaya
St Petersburg
Tel: +7 812 570 6700
http://www.comfort-hotel.org

Located close to the Admiralteyskaya Metro, the hotel is within walking distance to most of the city attractions and yet has a peaceful ambience. Opened in 2003, the guesthouse has 18 rooms in a refurbished century-old building. The hotel offers free parking, Wi-Fi, and other regular modern facilities. It has 24 hr reception and a travel desk.

There are 4 categories of rooms from the basic Deluxe to the Suite with a Jacuzzi. Room rates start from RUB 3800. There is complimentary tea and coffee.

Petro Palace Hotel

Malaya Morskaya Ulitsa 14
St Petersburg
Tel: +7 812 600 7075
http://www.petropalacehotel.com

Located just 150m from the Admiralteyskaya Metro, this
is a 4-star hotel with superb amenities in a prime location.
It is housed in an 8-storey historic building with 194
rooms. There is free Wi-Fi, a fitness center, a pool, and a
concierge desk. Rooms are equipped with iron, safety
box, mini-bar, and free mineral water. There is also a
solarium and a massage center.

Room rates start from RUB4500 with the lowest rate
guaranteed for online reservations.

Rentroom B&B

5. Sovetskaya Street 21
St. Petersburg
Tel: +7 812 923 0575
http://rentroom.ru/en/

This German B&B facility promises clean and safe rooms right at the heart of the city's attractions. It is housed on the 2nd floor of a mid 18th century refurbished building. There is free parking. The rooms are spacious with restored wooden flooring. In order to preserve the original form of the building, none of the rooms are ensuite although the management may reserve a bathroom for the guest during the non-peak season. The place has a common kitchen and free Wi-Fi.

Room rates start from RUB 3200 per person per night. There is a 10% surcharge in the month of June.

Old Vienna

13 Malaya Morskaya St
St Petersburg
Tel: +7 812 312 9339
http://vena.old-spb.ru/eng/

The Old Vienna Mini Hotel is housed in an early 20th century building and is located close to the Hermitage and other popular tourist attractions. This cozy hotel has a well stocked library for its guests, free Wi-Fi, a 24-hr café, a sauna, and a conference room, fax and photocopiers.

All rooms are ensuite and equipped with modern facilities including a DVD player and board games. Room rates start from RUB 3400.

Places to Eat & Drink

Zoom Café

Pea Street, Building 22
St Petersburg
Tel: +7 812 612 1329
http://www.cafezoom.ru

This cozy eatery serves European food in a cozy atmosphere, perfect for a relaxing meal after a hectic day.

Servings are large and half a dish is often enough for a single person. Reasonable prices with a multi-lingual staff are added advantages. Breakfast dishes start from RUB 60 and vegetarian salads from RUB 140. Vegetarian entrees (fried potatoes with mushrooms) start from RUB220 and non-vegetarian (beef steak with brandy) from RUB 460. It also serves a wide variety of alcohol. It is open from 9:00 am until midnight.

Romeo's Bar & Kitchen

Rimskogo-Korsakova 43
St Petersburg
Tel: +7 812 572 5448
http://romeosbarandkitchen.ru

This elegant restaurant is located opposite the Mariinsky Theater. Beautifully decorated interiors with a multi lingual staff make for a good first impression, which is backed up by deliciously cooked dishes of Russian and International cuisine. Menu includes salads (from RUB 260) and soups (from RUB 240). One can also try ethnic Russian dishes. Chicken entrée starts from RUB 390. The eatery also takes order for confectionary items. It has special set menus for pre and post theater dinners.

Chekhov

Petropavlovskaja ul, 4
St Petersburg
Tel: +7 812 234 4511
http://en.restaurant-chekhov.ru

Decorated in 19th century dacha, the Chekhov is one of
the best places to try authentic Russian cuisine. It is
recommended to make a reservation as this popular
restaurant is very busy, especially on weekends. There is
a wide variety of starters and fish and meat entrees.
Starters and soups start from about RUB350. Fish entrees
(fried fish with eggplant) and meat entrees (roasted pork
loin with cheese) start from RUB 600.

Tandoor Indian Restaurant

Admiralteisky Prospekt, 10
St Petersburg
Tel: +7 812 312 3886
http://tandoor-spb.ru/

The restaurant, located close to the historic avenue, has
made a name for itself serving North Indian cuisine. Hot
appetizers range from RUB 150 - 700. There is a wide
variety of tandoor (grilled) meat costing about RUB 600
each. The restaurant also serves a wide variety of
vegetarian items. The traditional Indian desserts cost
about RUB 150. There is a separate set lunch menu. It also
serves alcohol.

Stolle

Konushenny Lane 1/6
St Petersburg
Tel: +7 812 312 1862
http://www.stolle.ru

With over 20 branches all over Russia, it is one of the most popular lines of pie shops in the country. Varieties of pie include apple, cranberry, lemon, and apricot, to name a few. It also sells non-vegetarian pies including chicken, salmon, fish, and rabbit. It is a perfect place to grab a quick bite. It is open from 10:00 am to 9:00 pm.

Places to Shop

Dom Knigi

Nevsky Prospekt
St Petersburg

Located on the historic avenue, the Dom Knigi is a massive bookstore with one of the largest collection of books in the city. The travel section is specially recommended. The store is located in an ex-Zinger house – the famous sewing-machine company. There are books in many languages and of many categories and even if one is not planning to buy a book, it is worth a visit just for its sheer scale.

Galeria Shopping Mall

Ligovsky pr. 30A
St Petersburg
Tel: +7 812 643 3172
http://www.galeria.spb.ru/

The quintessential place for the shopaholic with 22 major
brands, 10 bowling alleys, and 10 cinema halls! Located
close to the historic center, it is the perfect place to relax
and shop during one of those short spells of rain that is
common in the city. The mall also has a food court to grab
a quick bite.

Artcity Souvenir Salon

Moyka River Embankment, 90
St Petersburg
Tel: +7 812 315 4676
http://artcitygroup.com/

This souvenir store is the perfect place for those who
want to buy some authentic Russian souvenirs without
wanting to go about hunting different stores for a variety
of products. One can buy dolls, jewelry, shawls, military
hats, traditional miniature boxes, and Russian military
emblems under one roof. This is also a great place to buy
those small easy-to-carry gifts.

Imagine Club Vinyl Records Store

Zhukovskogo St., 20
St Petersburg
Tel: +7 812 273 6159
http://imagine-club.com/

Russia is one of cradles of classical music and music lovers may want to bring back one of those musical souvenirs that has made so many Russian masters a quintessential favorite of music lovers all over the world. The Imagine-Club has a wide variety of rare and original vinyl records that is a must-visit for music lovers and collectors. Prices of these rare albums range from RUB1000 to over RUB11000! They also sell new CDs and DVDs.

Pushkinskaya 10 Art Center

53 Ligovsky Prospect
St Petersburg
Tel: +7 812 764 5371

Located opposite the Galleria shopping mall, this is a small labyrinthine gallery which is also a museum for non-conformist art. It is run by a group of artists so one can have a great conversation before deciding on any piece of art. It is open from 3:00pm to 7:00pm from Wednesday to Sunday.

Made in the USA
Middletown, DE
08 September 2017